8 Key Ingredients Needed For …

SUCCESS GOD'S WAY

John L. Benford

sermonto**book**
.com

Sermon To Book
www.sermontobook.com

Success God's Way / John L. Benford
ISBN-13: 9780692354988
ISBN-10: 0692354980

I dedicate this book to all of my church family, spiritual sons, daughters and all of the men and women of God who have modeled godly success in my presence. To those who will read the pages of this book and dare to make their life's quest to have success God's way, you're a born-again winner. May the pages of this book impart revelation, insight and faith that causes you to endure adversity in order to achieve good success in life.

CONTENTS

How To Succeed God's Way

This probably won't come as a surprise, but not all success is godly success. Thousands of people find success with illegal methods. True, they might own a mansion on the moon, but they lack the most important thing on earth: God's blessing.

In this book, you will discover how to find success God's way. To do that, you have to make a choice. Will you commit to being all that God has created you to be … or live a life of mediocrity? Now, I don't need to tell you that living for God is challenging, but He will shower you with success and blessing if you do. Psalm 84:10b: "The Lord bestows favor and honor, No good thing does he withhold from those who walk uprightly."

The Key Ingredient

The key ingredient to finding success God's way is through constant saturation and mediation on God's Word. Joshua 1:8 says, "This book of the law shall not depart out of thy mouth; but thou shalt meditate therein day and night, that thou mayest observe to do according to all that is written therein: for then thou shalt make thy way prosperous, and then thou shalt have good success."

God is telling Joshua that if he would just focus by meditating on His Word and observe to do it, He will pour blessings on his life. And He will do the same for every believer who meditates and observes to do His Word. You see, it's not enough to simply read the Bible.

Difference Between Knowing and Doing

Although God told Joshua to meditate on the scriptures day and night, He also tells him, "You must observe to do it all." When you read the Word, your mind gets established in the right direction for godly success.

What is the benefit of knowing the Word but not living the Word?

There's a huge difference between *knowing* what God says and *doing* what He says. What is the benefit of knowing how you should live if you don't go out and live that way? You must allow the Word to penetrate into your heart and every area of your life for maximum benefit and blessings. God's commands must affect your thoughts, your words, your decisions, your relationships, and so on. If you do that, God promises that you will prosper and have good success.

Some people wait on God to make their ways prosperous, but God says *you* will make your way prosperous. There's no denying that the power and the grace of God will permeate your life. But the bottom line is, you have to exert purposeful effort on your behalf to make your life successful. If you don't, you're never going to have the success that God wants for you.

Not Everything in Life is Profitable

Just because something is lawful doesn't mean it benefits you. In 1 Corinthians 6:12, Paul says, "All things are lawful for me, but not all things are profitable. All things are lawful for me, but I will not be mastered by anything."

Living outside of God's will is not fun. There are people in the world who have achieved all kinds of success (i.e. fame, money, notoriety), but not success God's way and they're miserable with life.

That verse is the reason this book is titled *Success God's Way*. If God doesn't want you to have something, don't push it. You might not agree with me, but living outside of God's will is not fun. There are people right now in the world who have achieved all kinds of success, (i.e. fame, money, notoriety), and they're miserable with life. Just because they have success doesn't mean it's good success. Once again, there is a difference between the world's definition of success and God's definition of success.

How many of your favorite musicians and television stars are addicted to fame, sex, drugs, and alcohol? The sad truth is that the majority of celebrities live that way, all the while claiming that they're living the good life. But the reality is that they are empty inside. And they know it.

Worldly celebrities might experience life in flashy colors, but what will it amount to in the end? Matthew 16:26 says, "For what is a man profited, if he shall gain the whole world, and lose his own soul? Or what shall a man give in exchange for his soul?"

Your Success is God's Idea

Are you struggling with the idea that God actually wants you to succeed? If so, ask Him for revelation. Because the truth is, no one wants you to succeed more than He does. This is all His idea, His plan. If you don't embrace that, you will constantly question how high you can go. In the book of the beginning, Genesis, we find that success was the created intent of God. After God created all things and bless it he called it good. Then he formed man and blew the breath of life into him and said, "be fruitful and have dominion and subdue the earth". Then God commended man to eat of everything but the tree in the middle of the garden known as the tree of the knowledge of good and evil. With these two instructions, God gave man the legal right to rule and reign over all his creation, to successfully manage and control everything. The command was to successfully lord over all of God's creation, doing it successfully, His way.

Now, let's find out what God has in store for you.

A Note From The Author

This book came together as the result of a message that I've shared with my church family. As I have observed the lives of people, I realized early on that their desire for success has not always been the type of success that others and I should desire or model because it has not been good or godly success. As I reflect over my life, my spiritual mentor Bishop IV Hilliard prayed over me "that God's promised best would be mine." I remember thinking, what is true success? After meditating and praying, the Lord showed me what godly success was. I believe that all who read this book and put these principles into practice will experience success God's way in their life forever. Amen!

CHAPTER ONE

Prosperity Is Not A Sin

Sadly, many believers think that God keeps people in poverty in order to teach them humility. False! God didn't send His Son to die on a cross so that His children would be poor. He said, "I took your poverty so that you might be rich."

Lots of believers will say, "I don't want to be prosperous because I may become prideful." You can be prideful and homeless or a prideful millionaire. The heart remains just as prone to pride, regardless of circumstances. Perhaps a reason for this type of thinking is a misunderstanding of what prosperity truly is! The root of the word prosperity is the word prosper which means success, the same word used in Joshua 1:8. True prosperity is having success God's way.

The Detriment of Accepting Ungodly Counsel

Psalm 1:1 says, "Blessed is the man that walketh not in the counsel of the ungodly."

Blessings are part of the benefit package for the believer. God says in Psalms that if we want good success, we need to understand where our blessings lie..

If you understand where your blessings lie , you can receive the benefits of those blessings and begin to achieve the success that God wants you to have.

When you need counsel, call a man or woman of God, someone who hears from above, someone who will offer you real spiritual wisdom, not a bunch of liberal gibberish. Do not take all of your advice from talk show hosts and self-help books.

If you're ever going to grow to receive what God wants you to do, you cannot live a hypocritical life. When you say that you are God's child, but you live like the world, you are a hypocrite and you're standing in the way of sinners.

Association Influences Decisions

It's commonly known that people will begin to act like whomever they associate with. That's why you'll hear moms say to their kids, "I don't want you running around with those boys. They are up to no good."

Because parents know that even though kids may not be doing what their friends are doing, eventually they will influence their decisions.

The Bible says, "But his delight is in the law of the Lord." The word "delight" means to take pleasure in doing the will of another. Sometimes in order to make God happy, you have to deny yourself. You have to say, "Not my will be done but Thy will be done."

In Mark 14:36, Jesus says, "Abba, Father, all things are possible unto Thee; take away this cup from me: nevertheless not what I will, but what Thou wilt."

He delighted in doing the will of the Father who sent Him.

Sometimes you don't need to know how God's Word works, you just need to have faith that it does. The Bible said it's like a man who sows seed in his garden. He knows not how it works, but one day he sees a harvest.

Sometimes you have to cut friends loose—sometimes even family members too. I'm not saying that you disassociate them from being in the family. When you go back home to the family reunion, you can't say, "I'm sorry, I can't hang out with you; I'm only here to eat some barbecue then I'm headed back home."

And then your cousin will say, "Oh, you think you're somebody now that you're down there in northwest Arkansas. Yeah, we know where you're really from."

They make you feel bad, don't they? And then they'll bring up all your dirt. They'll say, "Remember when we did this?" And then they'll say, "Now here, take a swig of this."

Have Faith That God's Word Works

Sometimes you don't need to know how God's Word works, you just need to have faith that it does. The Bible says it's like a man who sows seed in his garden. He knows not how it works, but one day he sees a harvest. First he sees a seed, then the blade, then the corn, then the full ear of corn in the husk. Then he takes the sickle for the harvest.

You would do well to take this metaphor to heart. Be faithful to sow your seed, day in and day out, and God will be faithful to make it come to pass. God says if you do this, you shall be like a tree planted by rivers of water.

The Components of a Good Tree

Trees gravitate to the water source, and their roots stretch out to receive the water and the nutrients. When the roots reach out, it establishes the foundation of the tree.

And as the foundation of the tree is established, it begins to grow taller and produce fruit. But it's impossible for a tree to produce good fruit without good roots. And so you have to be planted by a good watering source.

In other words, you need to attend a church that preaches the unadulterated Word of God in season and out of season. You need believers in your life who will tell you the truth, even to your own shame and hurt. You need to surround yourself with people who will look you in the eye and say, "You know I love you, but that isn't right. That's not good. You're not going to get the maximum out of that."

The Definition of Success

Success is the obtaining of a goal with the capacity to enjoy both the quest and the acquisition. You are not successful if you can't enjoy both the journey and the achieved goal.

According to Joshua 1:8 and Psalm 1, success is God's ideal; however, just because God wants you to be successful doesn't mean that it's automatically going to happen for you. God's plan must be pursued with purposeful, passionate effort.

You might be thinking, "If success is the will of God, why am I failing so badly?" That is a fair question. When things are not going your way, you must stop and ask the question, "What's wrong with this picture? I'm doing what God wants me to do. So, why am I not succeeding?"

If you're not succeeding, you need self-introspection. You have to look at yourself. You can't look at everybody else and blame your lack of success on them. If you don't like what you have, then change what you're doing. It's called personal responsibility.

According to Joshua 1:8 and Psalm 1, success is God's ideal; however, just because God wants you to be successful doesn't mean that it's automatically going to happen for you. God's plan must be pursued with purposeful, passionate effort.

It takes teamwork. God's going to empower you to succeed, but you still have a part to play. 2 Peter 3:9 says, "The Lord is not slack concerning His promise, as some men count slackness; but is longsuffering toward us, not willing that any should perish, but that all should come to repentance."

Don't be a slacker and let God do all the work. He's counting on you to seek Him like precious treasures.

Peter tells us that God is longsuffering. He is waiting for the hearts of men to change so that all will come unto repentance. Even so, not everyone will be saved. You have a part to play, even in your salvation. You have to pursue God. Don't be a slacker and let God do all the work. He's counting on you to seek him like precious treasures.

Matthew 6:33 says, "But seek ye first the kingdom of God, and his righteousness; and then all of these things shall be added unto you."

God said all of these things are available to you, but you must put forth some purposeful effort and seek out the kingdom.

CHAPTER TWO

Key Ingredient 1: Ability

Ability is your God-given natural gift. In order for you to achieve good success God's way, you need to know exactly what your abilities are. Just because you like something doesn't mean you necessarily have the gift for it. You may like singing, but that doesn't mean you have the gift. You may want to play in the NBA, but you're 4-foot-8.

Before you do anything else, you must discover your God-given gifting.

But maybe you have an innate ability to think analytically and logically, and you can come up with solutions that no one else can. Whatever your gift may be, hone that skill, knowing that God can use it as an ingredient for you to achieve success His way.

Before you do anything else, you must discover your God-given gifting. Deuteronomy 8:8 says, "Then thou shalt remember the Lord thy God: for it is he that giveth thee the power to get wealth, that you may establish his covenant which he swore to his fathers, as it is this day."

Once you discover your God-given ability, you must understand that God has not only given you your gift, but He has also given you the power to bring Him glory through it. Proverbs 18:6 says that a man's gift will make room for him and bring him into the presence of great men.

God has given us certain abilities, and once we develop those abilities, we will achieve success. An ability that is not mature will never develop to maximum success.

God says if you focus on your gift, He will take you into the company of the people that you need to keep. Once you understand that, you can begin to perfect the law of association.

God has given us certain abilities, and once we develop those abilities, we will achieve success. An ability that is not mature will never develop to maximum success.

Take LeBron James for instance. He has the gift and the talent to play basketball. But he said, "As I study San

Antonio, I realized that they were going under the pick and I was going to be open for the 17- and 15-footer. I've been shooting all year a high percentage. I realized if we were going to win the (championship) series, I was going to have to knock down the 15-17foot middle-range jumper."

He said that every pre-game and practice he would work on nothing but the 15-17-foot midrange jumper. And in the last game he shot his highest percentage. Because he understood he had to practice his gift until it was mature.

Just because you have a natural ability doesn't mean you should cease maturing your gift. Never act like you've arrived.

Just because you have a natural gift doesn't mean you can't improve on it. One of the greatest painters spent four hours painting every day, even when he was 85 years old. You have to make sure that you stay sharp at all times. Just because you have a natural ability doesn't mean you should cease maturing your gift.

Never act like you've arrived. God gives us the power to get wealth for the purpose of establishing His testimony in the earth.

When you really desire to be successful for the glory of God, then He says He will use you. If you want to become successful for the sole purpose of showing everybody what you can do, God says your purpose is not right. The purpose of your heart is not for personal gain. It's to give God praise.

When God brings you to the highest level, he says, "You didn't make it on your own. Remember, it is I who giveth you the power to get it."

CHAPTER THREE

Key Ingredient 2: Academics

Academia is the scholastic or spiritual information which will cause one to excel and advance. What you know will help you excel and advance. If academia is not obtained, it can cause one postponement of their plans, their dreams and their goals.

Now, how does God use academics to cause you to succeed the way He wants you to?

I venture to say that it is very strongly possible that you have not achieved what God has for you because of something you do not know.

Hosea 4:6 says, "My people are destroyed for lack of knowledge. They're destroyed for lack of knowledge, because thou hast rejected knowledge."

Why were they destroyed? Because they rejected the knowledge that was available to them. And because of that, God said, "I have also rejected thee." Thus, it was important for them to be partakers of the knowledge that God had for them.

I venture to say that it is very strongly possible that you have not achieved what God has for you because of something you do not know.

'What you don't know can't hurt you.' That is a flat out lie. The truth is, what you don't know can kill your future and your dreams.

Which leads me to the old adage that we often hear: what you don't know can't hurt you. That is a flat out lie. The truth is, what you don't know can kill your future and your dreams. So work to glean all the knowledge and information you can, especially the knowledge that pertains to the subject you want to succeed in.

If you want to succeed at something, get all the information that you can in order for God to be able to use that ingredient to help you succeed His way.

If you shun the information that is available to you, don't be upset if success is derailed or postponed. God said that because you rejected the knowledge that was available to you, He has rejected you.

When you ignore knowledge, you gain ignorance. Some say school is unnecessary. If it's available to you, go. Books and information that are available to you, read. If you ignore them, you will gain access to ignorance.

When you properly use the knowledge you've received, it translates into wisdom. You cannot become wise if you don't obtain the knowledge from the source of information. Information is key and we live in the information era.

When you properly use the knowledge you've received, it translates into wisdom. You cannot become wise if you don't obtain the knowledge from the source of information. Information is key and we live in the information era.

We are drowning with information, yet people are not becoming wiser because they are ignoring the information that is available to them.

When God wants to move you forward, He will always give you access to a person or information. And if you don't take advantage of either of those things, you will stay in ignorance.

Proverbs 24:3 says, "Through wisdom is a house built and by understanding is it established." Wisdom takes the knowledge gained from the information, and then it constructs something out of it.

When you understand how the wisdom works to your advantage, you will establish something in your life. When you learn how to make money, it doesn't matter where you are, you can make it.

Ignorance will cause you to be retained at the level that you presently occupy. Letting the world of technology and advancement pass you by will cause you to become ignorant and it will cause you to continue to occupy where you are.

Donald Trump can go bankrupt and I can bet that in no time at all he'll rebuild it. Because he has understanding of the wisdom from the knowledge that he has gained from information and access to people, to books, to places, and things.

Therefore he's able to establish a financial future because of his understanding about how money flows and how money works. I'm just using him as an example, whether he's Christian or godly or not.

Ignorance will cause you to be retained at the level that you presently occupy. Letting the world of technology and advancement pass you by will cause you to become ignorant and it will cause you to continue to occupy where you are.

I'll be honest with you. I have not always been a big proponent of social media. But I realized that I must begin to take advantage of this technological advancement. If not, I'm at fault for not advancing toward greater success in my life.

It's okay if you don't understand everything about technology. If you can't tweet, find somebody who can.

Although I don't like tweeting and Facebooking, I'm going to have to get with it because if I don't, I may find myself left behind. It's okay if you don't understand everything about technology. If you can't tweet, find somebody who can.

If social media intimidates you, ask God to help you, saying, "God give me access to the people that I need to have in my life to help me accomplish whatever your goal and your plan is." You ought to pray that, too, no matter where you are in life.

Let's discuss 3 things that you can learn from taking advantage of technology or information that is available through this process of academics.

1. Resourceful

We need to learn to be resourceful in the way we acquire knowledge and information to help our success along life's journey.

2. Resolve

We need to have resolve. We have to know how to stick with it and complete a task. Often, many of us don't have resolve, therefore we don't complete much. First, learn to start with the small stuff.

Starting is one thing, but finishing it is another. God said that it is the small foxes that spoil the vine.

My wife and I work to teach our children how to have resolve. We teach them the importance of learning how to complete a task. It's easy to get in the habit of starting and not finishing. We start school but don't finish. Or we start a book but don't finish.

You may start a project like cleaning the garage and didn't finish it, and the garage has remained unfinished for the rest of the year. Starting is one thing, but finishing it is another. It's the small foxes that spoil the vine, Song of Songs 2:15

Resolve means that when you start something, you see it to completion. It doesn't matter how resolved you are, you can always have better resolve. We all can better ourselves by having a greater resolve.

3. Responsibility

Responsibility means learning how to hold yourself accountable. Responsible people hold themselves accountable. A responsible person owns it.

I cannot blame my failures on you. I have to own that. I have to be responsible for me. No one controls your world but you.

You might not think your on-the-job training is doing anything for you. Yes it is. It's qualifying you to be used by God.

Don't let people hold you back, either. Information and academics is important. The apostle Paul told his protégé, Timothy, in 2 Timothy 2:15, "Study to show yourself approved unto God."

Note that Paul did not tell him, "Listen Tim, just because you are called, you don't have to worry about anything. God is just going to download it." No, he said, "Study. Prove that you're qualified to be used by God." Academics qualify you to be used by God.

You might not think that your on-the-job training is doing anything for you. Yes it is. It's qualifying you to be used by God. Don't shun away from the academics. God said a workman need not be ashamed but can rightly divide the word of truth.

When you study, it doesn't just show approval unto God; it shows you how to rightly use the information that you just learned. Any fool can quote Scripture and most do. And quote them out of context and out of time. And half say them wrong and swear they are right. But just because you can quote them doesn't mean that you know how to use them. God didn't tell us to quote Scripture; He said to live them. Let it be in your life. Let people see what God can do in your life.

I'm not impressed with somebody who can just quote a bunch of Scriptures. I need to see those Scriptures lived out in their lives.

I'm not impressed with somebody who can just quote a bunch of Scriptures. I need to see those Scriptures lived out in their lives. If you do that, God says that your life is an epistle, a written letter read among men. In other words, the Scriptures that you read make your life an open book for everyone to read. If that's so, then what is your book all about? Is it fiction? Nonfiction? A worldwide bestseller?

Acquiring knowledge is the most valuable asset you'll have in your quest for success. Luke 14: 28 says, "For which of you intend to build a tower and sets not down first, and counted not the cost whether you have sufficiency to finish."

In other words, your pre-learning makes you sufficient with the ability to finish. In sports, they call that pregame study. What a football player does on the field on Sunday—what makes him successful—is what he did in the pregame during the week by looking at film.

The Bible tells us constantly that we are not ignorant to the devil's devices. In other words, knowledge obtained about your adversary can help you be successful in life.

So these athletes are constantly studying film, gathering information on their opponent so they'll have knowledge in what to do and how to do it at a particular moment. That's how they have great success. Again, even in sports, information is used to gain knowledge over opponents.

The Bible tells us constantly that we are not ignorant to the devil's devices. In other words, are you getting any information or any knowledge on your adversary to help you be successful in life?

Finishing is the hallmark of success. The Bible says the race isn't given to the swift nor is it given to the strong. It is given to he who endureth to the end. Finishing is the hallmark of success.

It's not how you start but it's how you finish. In Hebrews 11, it talks about those in the hall of faith who have finished and have obtained the prize. The Apostle Paul talks about in 2 Timothy 4:7 "How he fought the good fight, he kept the faith and finished his course". We all must run our race, fight our fight and finish our course.

If you're not a finisher, He can't put maximum investment in you. And if He can't put maximum investment in you, then you're not going to be able to succeed God's way.

I want to be successful God's way. But if you're not a finisher, you'll never have godly success because God is not invested in quitters.

And if you are not determined to have resolve, God says you're probably not a finisher. And if you're not a finisher, He can't put maximum investment in you. And if He can't put maximum investment in you, then you're not going to be able to succeed God's way.

God is an excellent God. If you don't believe that, look at the world around you. And look at its beauty and splendor. It declares the majesty of our God.

As a matter of fact, finishing is so important that on the seventh day, God looked at all that He had done and He rested because all His work was good. After Jesus was on the cross, the last thing He said was, "It is finished." There is power in those three little words. Aren't you glad He didn't bow His head and say, "To be continued"?

He ascended to the Father and now sits at the right hand. And He looks at the work that He has done because Jesus is our prototype and He can say He has success God's way. In Hebrews 12:2a, Jesus is the author and finisher of our faith.

CHAPTER FOUR

Key Ingredient 3: Adaptability

If you're going to be successful in life, you're going to have to learn the law of adaptability. In 2 Kings 4:1-7, the wife of a prophet says, "Thy servant my husband is dead. And thou knowest that thy servant did fear the Lord: and the creditor is come to take unto him my two sons to be bondmen."

Let's take a look at this story to understand adaptability a little better. This lady was a godly woman and her husband was a prophet, yet look what happened:

1) **Death**: Her husband died unexpectedly.

2) **Debt**: They had an accumulation of creditors.

3) **Detention**: The authorities were going to imprison her two sons, the only family she had left. They would have to serve hard time until the debt was paid in full.

Assess Your Resources

The story shifts because the woman did something differently. She had to adapt to her situation midstream. She probably thought to herself, "I didn't want this, but if I don't adapt, it's over. So how do I get myself back on track?" And what did she do? She sought help from a man of God.

In life, unexpected difficulty, hardship and circumstances can come upon you immediately. The newly widowed woman came to Elisha for counsel, and Elisha said, "What shall I do for thee? Tell me," 2 Kings 4:2. Some people are too prideful to ask for wise counsel. That's foolishness. If you can't handle your problem, take it to somebody who can help with your problem.

When you have problems and you possess the law of adaptability, it produces answers in your life.

And that's just what she did. Elisha said, "Tell me, what you have in your house?" And she said, "Thine handmaid hath not anything in the house, except for a pot of oil."

He replied, "Go, borrow thee many vessels from all of thy neighbors, and empty all of the vessels; don't borrow a few. And when thou shall come in, shut the door on you and thy sons, and begin to pour into the vessels, and then set them aside which are full."

When you have problems and you possess the law of adaptability, it produces answers in your life. When you get a curveball thrown at you in life, don't run from God. Run to God. Don't leave church; go to church. Don't go to the club; come to church. Don't go to the drug man; come to church.

When unforeseen problems enter your life and you don't know how to handle it, the stress and the pressure pushes you over the edge. But that's okay. You're going to wake up and dry your eyes and say, "You know what? I have something working on my behalf. I have the ingredient of adaptability. I'm designed to succeed. I can adjust to this."

You will find out that when you get wise counsel and they give you an instruction, you will go back and see what you never saw before.

Elisha instructed the woman to assess her resources. You will find out that when you get wise counsel and they give you an instruction, you will go back and see what you never saw before. In other words, Elisha was able to speak into her life and she discovered previously unrecognized resources.

There is always more available to you than meets the eye. You may have never seen it before, but when somebody speaks into your life, it's like the veil is lifted.

You have more available to you than you know what to do with.

Unrecognized resources are often overlooked and discredited. Elisha says to her, "take inventory and assess what's around you." There are undiscovered and unrecognized resources available to you. You have more available to you than you know what to do with.

Don't ever discredit your little bits, because they can turn into much in the hands of God. In Matthew 14:17, Jesus fed 5,000 people with a little boy's lunch, yes, a two -piece fish dinner. God can use anything to bless His children.

As the disciples began to break the bread, it multiplied. Sometimes, a business starts out with a small amount of money, but if you just trust God, He will begin to slowly multiply it. Always remember that little becomes much in the hands of God.

Acquire From Those Around You

Somebody always has something to give. They have something they can offer you. You just need to know how to acquire from others that are around you.

There's nothing wrong with asking someone, "I was raised in the hood. How'd you get out? How did you do it, man? Tell me, what did you do? I used to be a hustler, but I don't want to hustle anymore. Tell me how you went straight. Help a brother out."

God will send somebody your way who will use their favor and their influence on your behalf. They'll give you what you need to help you along the way.

For those who are willing to offer what they have, it's because they're humble enough to know they didn't make it by themselves, but that God was on their side.

If you're going through a tough time or if you don't believe that God is going to show up somewhere, you'll surely lie down and quit. But if you just keep pushing on every single day, God can strengthen you.

God will send somebody your way who will use their favor and their influence on your behalf. They'll give you what you need to help you along the way.

Make sure when you borrow, you borrow with the intent to use it for what it was needed for. If God provides money when you need to pay a bill, don't spend that money frivolously. You should pay your bill.

Allocate the Asset to the Problem not your Pleasure

If you have debt, pay it off. Elisha gave the widow specific instructions to pay off her creditors, then live off of the rest of her money. He then warns her not to go into further debt, once she's out of debt.

If you succeed in getting out of debt, make sure that you don't revert to your old spending habits. This will only repeat the process.

When I say, "acquire from others," I'm not just talking about borrowing money. I'm talking about borrowing knowledge, wisdom, and life experience from others. Find people around you who can add value to your life. Learn from their experiences rather than learning life's lessons the hard way.

CHAPTER FIVE

Key Ingredient 4: Attitude

In Judges 6, there's a story about a man named Gideon. Gideon was a young man who basically had an inferiority complex. Gideon also had what was known to be a negative or pessimistic attitude towards the things of life and God.

Judges 6:8-10 says, "Do not be afraid of their god for I am the Lord God that is with you." It goes to show that even though God can deliver us from some things, that doesn't mean that we're not going to have some battles in our life to fight.

When God delivers us, we will still have battles in our lives. But God said whatever it is that you're coming up against, don't fear it because He says, "I have given you the power to overcome, but your attitude must be correct."

Verse 10 says, "I say unto you, I am the Lord your God; don't fear the god of the Amorites, in whose land you dwell, but you have not obeyed my voice."

A lot of times, when we are not prospering in God's promised blessing, it is because we live a disobedient lifestyle or we disobey the voice of God. Sometimes our defeat is because we're not walking in obedience to the voice of God. God never delivers us to allow us to be defeated.

Verses 14-16 says, "Go in this might of yours, and you shall save Israel from the hand of the Midianites: I have sent you."

How you respond to adversity (i.e. your attitude) shows everybody else what you really think.

He comes to Gideon and says, "Gideon, you're a mighty man of valor." The Bible says that Gideon was in the press and he was hiding. Now God had delivered His people and He says they were living in caves and they were hiding. And the enemy would always come in and destroy everything that they worked for.

Sometimes when God delivers us, the enemy is destroying our life because we're in hiding. Not only are we in hiding, but we're in hiding because we're not obeying God's voice.

And so He says, "Now I'm going to call you a mighty man of valor."

He says "I want you to go in this might that I'm giving you, for I have sent you". Verse 15 says, "So he said unto him, 'Oh, my Lord, how can I save Israel? Indeed my clan is the weakest in Manasseh.'"

Gideon was born out of the tribe of Manasseh, and he said that his family was the weakest of the tribe. This is showing you the attitude that Gideon has about who he is and what he has and the inability of his family.

A lot of times, we think God is against us, but in reality, we're just not obedient to His voice.

His attitude is already inferior. He goes on and says, "And the Lord said unto him, surely I will be with thee, and you shall defeat the Midianites as one man." Now, in order for Gideon to have success God's way, he needs an attitude adjustment.

God comes to him and calls him a mighty man of valor. But Gideon says, "I'm the smallest in the household, and then I'm the weakest in my own family."

In other words, he's the runt out of the bunch. But God says, "I commanded you to go in the might and the calling that I have on your life". Verses 23-24 says, "So Gideon built an altar to the Lord and he called it the Lord is Peace. To this day it shall be in Ophrah of the Abiezrites."

Attitude is an emotional response to adversity when it is encountered and it becomes visible to others. That means when you encounter adversity, your attitude becomes visible to everybody else.

How you respond to adversity (i.e. your attitude) shows everybody else what you really think. Leaders learn to have a positive attitude and self-confidence in their ability to achieve what it is that God's calling them to do.

Don't underestimate the power of an obedient believer. Obedience is everything. We tie God's hands when we are disobedient to His voice.

Your attitude is the visible reflection of your faith when dealing with adversities of your life's challenge. When people are looking at leaders, their attitude is a visible reflection of their faith.

Gideon said that the Lord had done all these things for his family, but everybody was dominating them and taking them over. . It wasn't that the Lord was no longer with them; it's just that God says, "If you're not going to obey Me, I can't fight on your behalf." A lot of times, we think God is against us, but in reality, we're just not obedient to His voice.

Don't underestimate the power of an obedient believer. Obedience is everything. We tie God's hands when we are disobedient to His voice. It doesn't mean that

God doesn't want to work with us. It means God can't work when we're disobedient.

It's important not to crop up a negative attitude while trying to do life God's way. God wants you to assess where you are, check your attitude, and do it His way.

Some people don't like that, but it is the Word of God. God said, "I delivered you, but you have not been obedient, and because of this, you're suffering lack." To disobey God means to be separated from the power of God.

If you're separated from the power of God, He can't work on your behalf unless it's under just mercy. Sometimes mercy and grace can run out on you. His mercies are new every morning, but sometimes you feel like you don't have any more new mercy.

It's important not to crop up a negative attitude while trying to do life God's way. God wants you to assess where you are, check your attitude, and make sure that you're doing it His way.

Ephesians 4:31-32 says, "Let all bitterness and wrath and anger and clamor, and evil speaking, be put away from you, with all malice. And be kind to one another, tenderhearted, forgiving one another, even as God for Christ's sake has forgiven you."

Attitude is the most important ingredient to attain success God's way. It's hard for God to operate successfully in your life when you have a negative attitude.

Most folks need an attitude adjustment, because unfortunately, we have a lot of people who are bitter, talking evil. They're always angry and they're operating with malicious intent. This means they are operating with a negative attitude.

Attitude is the most important ingredient to attain success God's way. It's hard for God to operate successfully in your life when you have a negative attitude. He cannot pour new wine into old wineskins.

If you're going to be what God wants you to be and to succeed His way, you're going to have to adjust your attitude. How do you do that? You can use your emotions to trigger proper biblical responses to your various challenges and encounters.

When people do things and say things that cause you to have a negative attitude, work to respond in a biblical manner. If you use your emotions to trigger a proper biblical response, your attitude will be displayed differently.

If you use your emotions to trigger a proper biblical response, then it dis-

plays a different attitude. And that's why you must always be mindful of God's Word.

That's why the Bible says if one man slaps you, offer up the other cheek. If a man asks you to go one mile, go two. If you use your emotions to trigger a proper biblical response, then it displays a different attitude. And that's why you must always be mindful of God's Word.

Here are 3 things that a negative attitude will affect:

1. Your Decision Making Abilities

A negative attitude will always affect your decision-making. Don't make a permanent decision because of a temporary attitude problem. Always take a moment to gather yourself to think rationally about your current situation. Don't let anger rule your decision-making.

2. The Quality of Your Commitment

If your attitude is not correct, it will affect the quality of your commitment. Some people are not committed to the process long-haul because their attitude is not right.

People say, "I'm going to do this but _____." You see, they're planning on doing something, but their attitude is saying, "I really don't want to do this." That automatically calls into question the level of their commitment.

When we have an attitude adjustment, God begins to bless us overwhelmingly to where the blessing can be extended to others. That's what happens when we have an attitude adjustment.

We see this in counseling quite a bit, when we have couples therapy. The couple is angry at each other, and we tell them, "Well, what we want you to do is read the Word of God daily, and then begin to pray openly with one another."

And this is a very common response: "Well, I'm going to do it, but I really don't think it's going to help." Their attitude is negative already. It just doesn't make sense. Here they are, asking for counsel to overcome a problem, but they can't get the help they need until their attitude changes. Because it's going to call into question the level of commitment.

And they come back the next month, and we ask them, "Did you do what we asked you to do?" And they say, "Well, we did it for a couple of days, but we knew it wasn't going to work, and we didn't see any results, so we stopped." That tells us that their commitment was not there from the start.

A negative attitude not only affects your commitment, but it also affects how long you will remain committed.

Remember the story when Peter had been out fishing all night and he had caught nothing? And when Jesus came that morning, He saw Peter mending his nets. And then Jesus asked, "Can I use your boat ?"

Jesus got into Peter's boat and began to teach that morning's lesson to the people. And before Jesus was finished, he said, "Peter, drop your nets on the right side of the boat."

And Peter's response was, "Wait a minute, Jesus. I know you're the master teacher, but I am the master fisherman and the best fishing is at night. And we have fished all night, yet we caught nothing. But then he said, "Nevertheless, at Thy Word." At that moment, Peter changed his attitude. He did as the master said. And the haul of fish was so great, he had to call for his buddies who were around to come and help him.

When we have an attitude adjustment, God begins to bless us overwhelmingly to where the blessing can be extended to others. That's what happens when we have an attitude adjustment.

3. The Duration of Your Commitment

A negative attitude not only affects your commitment, but it also affects how long you will remain committed. God wants us to be committed to the process long-term. He says if He is the author of our faith, then He is the finisher of our faith. That means in the midst of trials and in the midst of trouble, we've got to stay committed.

Do you ever feel like giving up, throwing in the towel, or quitting? Somewhere along the line, you just say, "It's not working the way I thought it would."

Have you ever had something not go the way you thought it would? So you end up just cutting your losses? If you don't change your attitude, it's going to be a bumpy ride. God says, "If you'll change your attitude, you can see Me work."

How do you change your attitude? Philippians 2:5 says, "Let this mind be in you, which was also in Christ Jesus." When I search the Bible, Jesus always has the proper attitude. Never did you see Him have a negative attitude. His attitude was always correct. His response was always proper.

Two ways to change your negative attitude to mirror Jesus:

1. Only Say What the Father Says

Jesus only said what the Father said. The best way to change your attitude is to only say what the Father says. The doctor may say one thing, but I say what the Father says. If I say what everybody else says, then they influence my attitude. So I don't let them influence my attitude by their negative thinking and their negative comments. I just learn to say what the Father says. That's how Jesus had a proper response to everything. In other words, Jesus knew when to refrain or to react like the Father.

2. Please the Father Always

Jesus said, "I only do what I see Him do." That's an interesting statement. Jesus said, "I was with my Father from the beginning and I only reacted under adversity."

It's a challenge to have the proper attitude always, isn't it? But God says you're able.

In other words, when the angels betrayed Him, and one-third of the angels followed Lucifer, the Father reacted properly. His attitude was correct.

People who are able to function under a high level of adversity have a role model to teach them how to react. And so they react as they have seen someone else react.

God's strength is not always displayed in numbers. His strength is based upon His Word. When you start putting strength in numbers, God says you have missed the might of the call.

Men who grew up in a violent home where they saw their father physically abuse their mother because he could not handle pressure or adversity will grow up and react in the same way.

What have you been taught with your attitude, based upon what it is that you've seen? The attitude that Jesus always had was to always be pleasing to the Father. The Bible says, "Delight thyself in Me and I will give you the desires of your heart."

How do you do this? You change your attitude to where you want to delight yourself in the things of God. So that means that you must have the proper attitude always. It's a challenge to have the proper attitude always, isn't it? But God says you're able.

God's Might is Not Displayed in Numbers

Remember when 33,000 men showed up to fight with Gideon? Gideon's response was, "Man, I think the Lord is really moving on my behalf because I have all these people to back me up and help me go down here to fight."

But then the Lord told him, "You have too many people whose attitude is not the same as your attitude." Then God sent them down to the river and said, "Those who lap in their hand like a dog, that's who you keep, but everybody else who puts their head down in the water, let them go."

And before it was all over, when Gideon asked who was afraid and one-third of them left, Gideon got down to 300 people. And the call of God had not yet changed. All of a sudden, Gideon didn't feel as mighty as he had before.

God's Word can give you the information and the credibility that you need to help you change the old attitude that you have.

God's strength is not always displayed in numbers. His strength is based upon His Word. When you start putting strength in numbers, God says you have missed the might of the call.

God told David, "Never number how many chariots you have." And David's one chief sin was that he said, "I can go in the battle." David caused a plague to come upon Israel. Because God says, "Strength is never based upon numbers."

Your might is based upon the Word of God. God has told you to do something and the strength is not in the numbers of your bank account; the strength is in the might of the call. God said, "If I called you to do it, your strength lies there."

Samson's strength was never in his hair. Samson's strength was in the might of the call.

Sometimes God has to allow you to hear what everybody else is saying about the attributes that you don't realize you have.

God is telling Gideon: "I want you to see this Gideon." Verse 10 says, "But if you are afraid to go down to the camp, go with Phurah, your servant, and you shall hear what they say and afterward your hand shall be strengthened to go down against the camp." Sometimes God has to allow you to hear what everybody else is saying about the attributes that you don't realize you have.

Verse 13 says, "And when Gideon came, there was a man telling a dream to his companion and he said, "I have had a dream. To my surprise, a loaf of barley bread tumbled into the camp of Midian and it came to the tent and it struck it so that it fell and overturned. And the tent collapsed."

Then his companion answered and said, "This is nothing else but the sword of Gideon the son of Joash, a man of Israel. Into his hand God has delivered Midian and the whole camp."

When Gideon heard the telling of the dream and its interpretation, he returned to the camp of Israel and said, "Arise, for the Lord has delivered the camp of Midian into our hand."

Here are 3 things that will correct a negative attitude:

1. New information from a reliable and credible source

When you want to change your attitude, you need to be able to access new information under a reliable and a credible source. God's Word can give you the information and the credibility that you need to help you change the old attitude that you have.

Gideon was able to go down and hear new information about what his enemy thought about him and that helped him to adjust his attitude to say, "We'll be well able to do this."

2. New experiences to replace bad experiences

All of Gideon's previous experiences were filled with defeat. But that's not the end of the story. When he over-hears his enemies talking about getting ready to be defeated by Gideon, he gained confidence. New experiences help him to overcome bad experiences. All it takes is a new experience and your attitude will change.

3) New benefits that far outweigh your original reservation

There are things that happen in life that cause us to have a negative attitude. But when God begins to tell you and show you that the benefits are going to far outweigh whatever reservations you have, you will feel your attitude beginning to change. And that's a beautiful thing.

See what God has not only done, but also what He is doing.

Your attitude will start to say, "Well, maybe God is going to do something in my life. Maybe it will work out better than I expected."

Some of you are not doing things that God has called *you* to do because you have the bad attitude that it's not going work. All you need to do is listen to God say, "This is going to be so much better for you. This is going to be far greater than you ever thought." And all of a sudden, you can get a new attitude change.

See what God has not only done, but also what He is doing.

Assess your life. Don't just look back over your life and see what it is that God has done for you, but also look and see what He's doing now. It will help change your attitude.

Believe in Your Newfound Might

Your newfound might is the call of God that He has sent you in. The Bible says, "Gideon, you are a mighty man of valor. I have sent thee. I have called thee."

All Gideon had to do was rest upon that calling and he was able to tap into a new level of might. But in order for him to do that, Gideon had to have a new attitude.

If you're going to succeed God's way, you must have an attitude adjustment.

CHAPTER SIX

Key Ingredient 5: Accomplishments

Accomplishments are important. Isaiah 55:11 says, "So shall My word be that goeth forth out of my mouth. It shall not return to Me void but it shall accomplish that which I please. And it shall prosper in the thing whereunto I send it."

God said that when He speaks, He not only speaks with purpose but His Word performs or accomplishes something. He says that it's going to prosper; it's going to be successful.

We must accomplish things in our life. A person who has never accomplished anything usually lacks confidence.

And confidence is a key ingredient in achieving goals and dreams. Unfortunately, sometimes people see confidence as arrogance. This is false!

Accomplishments are the units by which you measure your steps of progress toward success. You may not be where you want to be, but the ultimate goal is to get there.

A lot of people believe that success happens instantaneously. Like, boom, you wake up tomorrow and you've made it. No. Success is never one giant step. It's a series of measurable goals by which we chart our progress.

If you're going to continue to move in that direction, you have to have some measurable accomplishments along the way. A lot of people believe that success happens instantaneously. Like, boom, you wake up tomorrow and you've made it. No.

Success is never one giant step. It's a series of measurable goals by which we chart our progress. The Scriptures teach about fruit that comes progressively, not instantaneously.

If you don't understand this, you will ultimately fall under the delusion that your current state is going to be counted as sufficient. The Kingdom of God is not instantaneous; it is progressive.

Mark 4:26-29 says, "So the Kingdom of God is like a man who should cast seed into the ground. And he shall sleep, rising day and night, and the seed spring up and grew but he knew not how." It wasn't important for this individual to know *how* the process worked. He just understood that it did work. God's process always works even when you don't think it's working. You just have to have faith.

Success comes in stages. If you look at some professional athletes that sign these multi-million dollar contracts, it appears as if they just busted onto the scene and got paid. No. Their success has come because of the accomplishments they have achieved over the span of their life.

You just don't go from the mailroom to the CEO boardroom. That's not reality. It sure would be nice if it worked that way, but most often it doesn't. Are there exceptions? Yes. But that's not the rule.

The same goes for the corporate world. You don't get to the highest level overnight. You get there because you work tirelessly over the course of a long period of time. Success does not happen instantaneously. It happens progressively.

You just don't go from the mailroom to the CEO boardroom. That's not reality. It sure would be nice if it worked that way, but most often it doesn't. Are there exceptions? Yes. But that's not the rule.

When you achieve instant success, you don't appreciate it like you would if you poured blood, sweat, and tears into a goal for years. Over time, you will learn to appreciate the struggle. I didn't say you will enjoy it, but you will appreciate it.

But when somebody just hands success to you and you put forth no purposeful effort, you have no measuring stick to value what you have.

That's why most children waste their inheritance. They don't understand its value, so they go out and blow it. It happens all the time.

Conclusion

The only success that immediately comes is harvest time. When Adam fell, God could have redeemed all of mankind instantaneously, but he didn't. He set the plan that He foreknew was needed.

Then He sent His Son thousands of years later, but before Jesus came the prophets. God's plan was progressive, and now you and I are in the family of God. Because God understands that the harvest comes progressively.

But He says that when it's time to harvest, then the angels will come and cut down the harvest and then it's time to reap. The Bible says that God is longsuffering so that none shall perish. But all that believe shall come unto the Kingdom of God.

God is longsuffering with mankind because He is waiting for them all to come into the knowledge of His dear Son Jesus. His plan is progressive. He declares the end from the beginning. The journey takes enduring patience and faith.

You're going to have highs and lows. There will be moments when you'll want to quit. But if you chart your accomplishments along the way, you will gain perspective.

Here are 4 progressive steps in order to master your accomplishments:

1. Set a goal

This is the most important element in order to achieve success. Without a goal, you will surely flounder.

2. Set a timeframe

Let's say you want to lose weight. Give yourself a timeframe (for example, lose 10 pounds in 30 days) and that way, you will have a set deadline that you're aiming for. If you don't have a time frame to guide you, you'll most likely lose the drive to reach your goal.

3. Stay on course

How are you going to get there? Not by simply imagining that you're 20 pounds lighter. No, you're going to change your eating habits, your restaurant choices, and you're going to start exercising more.

Do you know why most people give up when they're trying to lose weight? It's because they don't see any measurable accomplishment after the first week.

Then they get upset and say, "Shoot, I'm going to eat some cookies." And they quit because they did not have an accomplishment to help them. Nothing happens overnight. Understand that success is little accomplishments that are measurable to show progress. You've got to stay the course.

4. Chart your accomplishments

Write down your accomplishments along the way. When you lose one pound, write it down. It's an accomplishment. Give yourself a smiley face. Put it on the refrigerator. Feel good about it.

Small successes in life become stepping-stones for larger challenges.

Maybe the following week, you lose 3 pounds. Give yourself another smiley face and feel good about your progress. Some people don't know how to chart their accomplishments. And when the devil comes to you and tells you that it's not working, he'll make you feel bad. He'll show you everything that's not right.

Small successes in life become stepping-stones for larger challenges. You're never going to achieve the big accomplishment if you do not recognize the smaller successes that lead up to the big one.

In 1 Samuel 17:32-36, the Philistines have come and they have defied the armies of Israel. And all the men are afraid of the big warrior by the name of Goliath. And David is a young boy who is following his dad's instructions by delivering some lunch to his brothers who were fighting on the front line.

And all of a sudden, David encounters this opportunity to accomplish something great. David said to Saul, "Let no man's heart fail because of him." David is speaking to Saul, the main man, the king of the army. He says, "Thy servant will go and fight with this Philistine."

When you look back over your life, you see what God has done for you in the struggle. You have confidence that if God was faithful back then, He'll be faithful now.

And Saul says to David, "Thou art not able to go up against the Philistine to fight with him for thou art but a youth and he is a man of war from his youth." And David said to Saul, "Thy servant has kept his father's sheep." In other words, he says, "I know that I don't look like I'm fit for the job, but let me tell you my pedigree. Let me go back and recount to you my accomplishments that have prepared me for this moment."

David says, "I'm a servant keeping my father's sheep. And there was a lion and a bear that took a lamb out of the flock. I went out after him and I smote him and I delivered him out of the mouth. And when he rose up against me, I caught him by his beard and I smote him, and then I slew him. I have accomplished fighting the bear and the lion."

What is Saul's response? He says, "Listen, you are too little for him. He's too big for you." But David replies, "No, you don't understand. He's too big to miss."

David understood the importance of small accomplishments that led him to a much larger goal. And because he had charted his accomplishments along the way, he felt primed to fight Goliath, even when others didn't believe that he could.

He had the confidence in himself and in his God because he said, "For God delivered them into my hands." David says, "If God's in it, nothing is too difficult for God."

So it doesn't matter what the battle is. It just matters that you're faithful to God's call on your life.

And when you look back over your life, you see what God has done for you in the struggle. You have confidence that if God was faithful back then, He'll be faithful now.

So it doesn't matter what the battle is. It just matters that you're faithful to God's call on your life. And when you get that revelation, you will understand that your small successes have prepared you for your destiny. It's the small accomplishments that have made you and me ready for what God has planned for our lives.

When everybody else tells you that you're going to fail, all you have to do is tell them what God has done in your life.

When everybody else tells you that you're going to fail, all you have to do is tell them what God has done in your life. Then suddenly you realize that small accomplishments prepared you for your greatest battle and your destiny. Never underestimate your accomplishments.

I don't care if all your haters say that your accomplishments mean nothing. Don't let anybody despise small beginnings. Don't let anybody discredit your successes. Your successes help prepare you for where you're going tomorrow.

Every stepping-stone of success helps build a firm foundation of confidence and encouragement in what God can do. My confidence is not in me; my confidence is in my God. And it's not just in my God, but it's in what my God can do. And not only what He can do, but what He can do with me and through me.

When I'm doing it God's way, I have confidence that if a stay in the will of God, He's going to work everything out for my good. Sometimes when you're up against the wall and the adversary looks like he cannot be defeated, you have to say to him, "Wait a minute. God has been so good and God has been so faithful. He never changes. He's the same God today, tomorrow and forever. He will take care of me."

CHAPTER SEVEN

Key Ingredient 6: Adversity

According to the Webster's Dictionary, adversity is a condition of continued difficulty or adverse fortune. Notice it says "adverse fortune" not "missed-fortune." Misfortune means that you missed your fortune. Adversity can cause you to miss your fortune. That is the result of a person who is unable to handle adversity. Psalm 34:19 says, "Many are the afflictions of the righteous, but the Lord delivers him out of them all."

Many are the adversities of a righteous person, but the Lord delivers him out of them all. One of the greatest things that God desires is to be believed. When I say that I believe God, it means that I have faith in Him and His Word. Therefore, no matter what the adversity or affliction I may be facing, I know that there is a 'but.' There are always two sides to a 'but.' But the Lord delivers us out of them all.

You just need to continue to meditate in the Word, confess it to God, delight in His ways, and know that whatever the adversity is, God is going to still deliver you.

Trials and tribulations come so that our faith may be tested and come forth as pure gold. When you believe what God's Word says about your circumstances, amazing things will happen in your life.

1 Peter 1:7 is a powerful scripture that talks about the adversity of trails. The Bible says that adversity is the trying of our faith. Trials and tribulations come so that our faith may be tested and come forth as pure gold. When you believe what God's Word says about your circumstances, amazing things will happen in your life. In Proverbs 24:10, it says, "But if you faint in the day of adversity, your strength is small."

Fainting when pressure comes means that you're not strong enough to endure it, which means you have abandoned whatever you have placed your assurance in.

To a believer, nothing is too difficult. Nothing. I know that's hard to believe. But either you have faith in God's Word or you don't. In the Easy Reading translation, it says, "If you are weak in times of trouble that is real weakness."

What makes a person strong is not the lack of trouble, but on the contrary, it's his strength in time of trouble.

Some of us want to be strong, yet we don't want any trouble.

What determines that you're strong is that you're able to stand up when trouble comes. The Message says, "If you fall to pieces in a crisis, there wasn't much to you in the first place." WOW! That says a lot about how we respond to adversity.

When you experience a crisis and you're a child of God, you get to see your faith work for you.

When you experience a crisis and you're a child of God, you get to see your faith work for you. If you hold on, stay on the course, and continue to meditate and delight in God's Word, you'll see Him do something miraculous in your life. But the problem is that when the problem comes, many of us want to give up.

Adversity is opposition, resistance, or impedance. It hinders your progress and accomplishments of a life goal or dream. When I go golfing with my buddies and we come to a real tough hole, someone always says, "Pressure busts pipes." See, if you put enough pressure on the pipe and it gets weak, the pipes will burst.

In electronics, they use resistors to impede the flow of current. So when a hindrance comes, its goal is to impede your flow from success. The next time resistance or a hindrance comes, you just need to stand up and straighten your back and say, "You can't break my flow."

Natural Resistance

The world often paints a very pessimistic view about life. And if you get caught up in that pessimism, it will naturally create resistance for you. You will never see the good in anything. You will always look at the glass as half-empty and never half-full.

A person needs to be optimistic in order to overcome adversity. If you are pessimistic and adversity comes your way, you're probably going to fail. And adversity is an ingredient God can use for success God's way.

Supernatural Resistance

There is natural resistance and then there is supernatural resistance. This satanic hindrance can derail you from God's best. Now, not everything is satanic. The devil gets a bad rap for a lot of stuff. For instance, you might blame the devil when your microwave breaks. It's not the devil's fault. You've had your microwave for 10 years. You probably need to replace it.

When Daniel wanted to know the will of God concerning his people, he fasted and prayed for 21 days. And when the angel came, he told Daniel, "I had heard you the first day, but I was fighting the prince of Tyre."

You're always fighting the enemy of the inner you. In other words, things that somebody has placed on you that stifle your ability from achieving at a higher level.

Remember, as you endure various adversities in your life, you will sometimes encounter satanic resistance, especially when you're trying to do the will of God.

Internal Resistance

Internal resistance is one of the strongest forms of resistance. It emanates from a low self-image, which is the main ingredient for quitters.

You're always fighting the enemy of the inner you. In other words, things that somebody has placed on you that stifle your ability from achieving at a higher level. Somebody might tell you, "You're just like your _____." Or, "You'll never be able to do that because you can't even _____." I'm sure you can fill in the blanks.

Those statements can cause low self-esteem, which in turn causes internal resistance, so that when you try to do something outside your realm of comfort, all you will hear are those pesky voices, which will ultimately cause you to not achieve a goal or desire in your life.

Three Ways to Train Yourself to Overcome Resistance

1. Become better, not bitter

When you fall into adversity, learn to become better, not bitter. Invest in yourself. You may have to take some schooling. Go take some extra classes. Maybe you've been off the job market for a while. Sharpen up that resume. Buy new work clothes. Take confidence courses. But don't become bitter. If you do, you're sure to fail.

But when the adversity comes, invest in yourself. Maybe life hasn't gone well and you find yourself single after being married for 20 years. Don't get bitter. Make yourself better. Go get a manicure, a pedicure, a full-body massage. Get it all whipped up. Get your two sets of spanx and pull them up high. It's possible they have spanx for men now.

2. Pay the price

What do I mean by pay the price? Work twice as hard. Be smarter and train harder than your competitors.

3. Go the extra mile

Give life your all. Be willing to do more in order to become more. I'm going to share a personal testimony with you about being disliked by an authority figure, (for example, a parent, a boss, or an instructor). This kind of adversity has the potential to keep you from accomplishing a goal or desire in your life.

How I Overcame Adversity

I had just graduated high school and my dream was to go to a Division 1 college, graduate and play in the NBA.

I had told my mother, "Don't worry. I got this all locked up. I'm the best in our town. I got it."

She said, "What you going to do if it don't work?"

I said, "You don't have to worry about it, Mom. I got this. You don't know how good your boy is."

Unfortunately, I didn't get an offer from the college of my dream. I wanted to play for UCLA, or DePaul just to name a few.

In my head, I could hear a relative say, "You'll never make it. You think you're all that. You're nobody. You're going to be right back here with us soon enough."

And she said, "Well, I tell you what. If it doesn't work, I want you to meet with this guy. I hear computers and electronics is going to be the thing."

I said, "Mom, I don't need that." But as fate would have it, my dream of being a professional NBA player was on hold and Technical College was the new direction. And I got into my car and drove 60 miles away from home to the big city of Indianapolis.

I felt like a small fish in a big pond. I'll never forget my first day in class. I sat in the very back row in the very left corner. I had cornrows in my hair. I had on my best slacks and my best shoes. The only person of color in my class and a few in the whole graduating class of several hundred people.

I remember my instructor looked over at me and said, "Benford, we don't want any trouble out of you." As he held up a KKK medallion laughing, acting as though he was kidding, I knew he was serious. The whole class started laughing. And it set fear in me because I was the only one of color. Nobody looked like me. I felt all alone. I was out of my surroundings.

Midway into the first semester, I got called in and placed on academic probation. The dean had originally planned to expel me. I had a .9 GPA because I was afraid to ask my instructor for help.

When the dean said he was going to expel me, in my head, I heard my auntie say, "You'll never make it. You think you're all that. You're nobody. You're going to be right back here with us soon enough."

I'll never forget, I fell on my knees and I said, "Please sir, whatever you do, don't send me back. I'll be labeled a failure. I'll do whatever I need to do."

And he said, "I tell you what, you have to get your grades up to a 2.0 before the end of the semester. If you do, I'll let you stay."

That's when I said to myself "It was time to invest in myself. It was time to work harder than ever before. It was time to pay the price."

The very next class period, I moved from that back row to the front. I sat between a 3.9 student and a 4.2 student, and I ended up making friends with them. We even started hanging out.

I came from a .9 to a 3.5, all because of God's grace in my life. So, don't be a quitter. Know that all things work together for good, even your trials.

Not only did I pass the class, I graduated with honors to earn my degree in electronic engineering and technology. I came from a .9 to a 3.5 GPA because of God's grace in my life. So, don't be a quitter. Know that all things work together for good, even your trials. Adversity is commonplace in the life of the believer but we're overcomers in the game of life.

You Are Born Again to Overcome

If you are a believer, you are born again to overcome. The whole purpose of you being born again is to overcome. 1 John 5:4 says, "For whatsoever is born of God overcometh the world. And this is the victory that overcometh the world, even our faith."

If you're born again, your faith will cause you to overcome. Faith is an ingredient that God has given to the born again believer that will cause you to overcome every situation of adversity and resistance in your life. You just have to tap in to that ingredient.

Learn to Identify with Christ

Hebrews 12:2 says, "Looking unto Jesus who is the author and the finisher of my faith." If faith is the victory that overcomes the world, all you need to do is identify yourself in Christ and develop your faith. Then you will automatically overcome adversity.

The Authority of the Believer

You have authority as a believer. Luke 10:19 says, "Behold, I give you power to tread upon serpents, scorpions and over all the power of the enemy." Even when you're battling satanic resistance, God has given you the power to overcome it. When you identify your faith with Christ, there's nothing you can't conquer.

Conclusion

Adversity can become the ammunition for the believer to achieve greatness and to accomplish God's best in their life.

So when you see adversity, the first thing you have to tell yourself is, "Adversity is nothing but ammunition to help me overcome in life. It will only make me better because I have faith that I can overcome whatever the trial is."

CHAPTER EIGHT

Key Ingredient 7: Assertiveness

Assertiveness is characterized by a bold or confident behavior. When God wants you to be assertive, He wants
you to be bold. One of the synonyms for assertive is ag-
gressive. God uses assertive people. For the will and the
plan of God for your life to come to pass, you have to be
assertive, bold, courageous, and strong.

That's what God commanded of Joshua when he led
everyone over the Jordan. Unfortunately, believers often
think that assertiveness leads to pride and self-
centeredness. But if you are passive about the will of
God for your life, it will never come to pass. God uses
assertiveness.

Passionate Patience

Patience is the ability to continue doing what is right
when it appears not to be working. Oftentimes, people
feel that patience means being passive. God wants us to
be patient. He wants us to constantly pursue what we

know is right until change comes. Hebrews 10:35 says, "Cast not away your confidence for it has recompense of reward."

Be Bold

When you're bold, it means that you're confident in what you know. When you confidently know the Word of God, you should be assertive about obeying it. And your assertiveness produces rewards.

Faith is the confidence and assurance of things hoped for. Faith passionately pursues the things of God. That's how we become successful doing it God's way. You must aggressively pursue God's will with all your might.

Don't let your confidence pass away. When things are not working, it causes you to lose your patience and give up. That's why many of us don't receive God's blessings in the area of faith.

Faith is the confidence and assurance of things hoped for. Faith passionately pursues the things of God. That's how we become successful doing it God's way. You must aggressively pursue God's will with all your might.

When we were growing up, we had a saying that went like this: "He hit him with all his might." It means that he didn't hold anything back. When we want God's will to come to pass in our lives, we have to passionately pursue it with all our might.

A fool operates in a multitude of words. All he does is talk about doing something. Have you ever known people who always say, "Child, I'm going to do this and I'm going to do that," but they never actually do anything.

You have probably been told, "If God wants you to have it, then you'll have it. Don't worry about it. It'll happen in time. Just sit back and relax." And 20 years passes, and you're still waiting for the will of God to come to pass in your life, and you wonder why it hasn't happened yet. The reason it hasn't happened is because you're not functioning in one of the key ingredients that God uses mightily: assertiveness.

Ecclesiastes 5:3 says, "For a dream comes through multitudes of business, and a fool's voice is known by a multitude of words." In other words, God may choose to answer your cry in a million different ways, but the point is that you are assertively pursuing His will, trying to see how He is going to bring your prayers to pass.

A fool operates in a multitude of words. All he does is talk about doing something. Have you ever known people who always say, "Child, I'm going to do this and I'm going to do that," but they never actually do anything?

There are lots of people like that. They talk loud but say nothing.

The Bible calls them fools. They're not assertive. They're passive.

One of the most difficult challenges to be successful God's way is getting started. And you cannot get started if you're not assertive.

And you know you can't get anything done that way. You can sit there and say, "Boy, I sure am hot. Let me get up and shut the front door." But you keep sitting there. And then 10 minutes later, you say, "I sure am hot. If that door was closed, it'd be cooler in here. I'm going to get up and shut the front door."

But you don't. An hour goes by. You say, "Boy, it sure is hot in here. There are flies in here and everything. Boy, it sure is hot. I just need to get up and shut that door. I don't know who left that screen door open."

Five o'clock comes and you say, "Child, it's been hot in here all day. I mean, they're flies in here. The screen door's been left open. Child, I should've gotten up and shut that screen door."

That's an example of saying a bunch of words without following through with them. That screen door can't shut itself. You have to get up and shut it yourself.

It's easy to understand that shutting the front door keeps flies out, but many of us don't understand how to keep the flies out of our lives. We don't assert ourselves to do what God tells us to do to close certain things off.

3 Steps to Obtaining Godly Success

1. Getting started

One of the most difficult challenges to be successful God's way is getting started. And you cannot get started if you're not assertive. A lot of times we may know what God wants us to do, but we just don't know how to do it, which leads to becoming passive. Then procrastination invades our lives, which leads to a lack of confidence.

2. Staying focused

Staying focused is essential to getting the maximum results out of your efforts. Where there is clarity of vision there is acceleration to the goal. A person who is focused receives maximum clarity. Once there is clear vision you can accelerate to the goal.

When you're driving your car, you know exactly how long it will take you to reach your destination. You know the route. You know every pothole. But if you have inclement weather and fog rolls in, then all of a sudden your speed slows to a crawl, when in normal conditions, you'd be going 60 miles an hour. The reason you slowdown is because you do not have clarity of vision, thus, you cannot accelerate and reach your destination quicker.

Staying focused is one of the major challenges in trying to be successful God's way. We must cast off everything that diverts our attention.

When God gives us vision and clarity, we have the ability to accelerate and reach our destiny in a timely fashion. Staying focused is one of the major challenges in trying to be successful God's way.

We must cast off everything that diverts our attention. When God wants to do something in our lives, we oftentimes get distracted. Old problems seem to pop up out of the blue; things you thought you had dealt with unexpectedly reenter your life. People you haven't heard from in years will all of a sudden contact you, and you'll say, "I thought that rascal was gone." It's a challenge because the enemy knows when you're succeeding, and that's when he wants to derail you. That's just how it works.

3. The Reward

If you can get started and stay focused, that's when your hard work pays off. Ask any mother who has experienced the pains of childbirth, and she'll tell you that the hard work of laboring was worth the reward of a newborn child.

God's plans for your life come with painstaking effort. Just because it is His will for your life doesn't mean it will happen effortlessly. And if you aren't assertive, you will find yourself in a position of suspense where nothing is working.

Sacrifice is Essential to Inherit God's Will

You must be willing to sacrifice along the way in order to have godly success. Even though God is in it, it does not mean that you're not going to have to sacrifice some things.

If you want to inherit the will of God, you must make sacrifices in your life.

A lot of times when God wants to do something in our lives, we feel that it's just going to happen automatically without sacrifices. We've deceived ourselves because the sacrifices are many. Even Yeshua knew that when He went to the cross, He had to make sacrifices, the first thing being His will. If you want to inherit the will of God, you must make sacrifices in your life.

Tyler Perry's Biography

Tyler Perry's inspirational journey from the hard streets of New Orleans to the heights of Hollywood's A-list is the stuff of American legend. Born into poverty and raised in a household scarred by abuse, Tyler fought from a young age to find the strength, faith and perseverance that would later form the foundations of his much-acclaimed plays, films, books and shows.

It was a simple piece of advice from Oprah Winfrey that set Tyler's career in motion. Encouraged to keep a diary of his daily thoughts and experiences, he began writing a series of soul-searching letters to himself.

The letters, full of pain and in time, forgiveness, became a healing catharsis. His writing inspired a musical, I Know I've Been Changed, and in 1992, Tyler gathered his life's savings and set off for Atlanta in hopes of staging it for sold out crowds. He spent all the money but the people never came, and Tyler once again came face to face with the poverty that had plagued his youth. He spent months sleeping in seedy motels and his car but his faith—in God and, in turn, himself—only got stronger. He forged a powerful relationship with the church, and kept writing.

In 1998 his perseverance paid off and a promoter booked I Know I've Been Changed for a limited run at a local church-turned-theatre. This time, the community

came out in droves, and soon the musical moved to At-
lanta's prestigious Fox Theatre. Tyler Perry never
looked back.

I heard Bishop Jakes tell the story that he has been
around the world and has dined with royalty. He has seen
some of the most elegant places. He says but when Tyler
Perry invited him to his house, he said, "I ain't never
seen anything as elegant." He said in the foyer, there's a
huge picture of him sleeping in his car. And from that a
series was birthed called Seeds of Greatness. He says he
began to weep as he looked at the picture. And back in
the car, he asked, "Did you know that all of this was in
you?" And he said yes.

Are you assertive enough and patient enough to continue even at the lowest point in your life when you've
sacrificed everything? Do you have what it takes to
move forward and achieve the maximum success that
God has in you?

Conclusion

Although you may have to sacrifice much to pursue
your dream, you should never sacrifice your spiritual
service. There have to be some things that you're not
willing to do.

Although it had not worked for him, Tyler's relationship with the church remained constant. If you're going
to have success God's way, you're going to have to be
plugged in at a church. You're going to have to get good

spiritual counsel. You're going to have to be around people who love and care for you. You have to be around people who can speak into your life. This is essential.

If you're going to have success God's way, you'll never have to exchange your soul in order to do it. You will never have to put down God's Word or godly living in order for you to be successful.

Although you're willing to sacrifice a lot, be careful how much. There are some who grow up in the house of God who have a gift and they take their gift and use it for ungodly purposes. And although they become mega successful, they don't have success God's way. They sacrifice everything and it costs them everything.

Matthew 16:26 says, "For what profit is it to a man if he gains the whole world and loses his own soul? Or what will a man give in exchange for his soul?" Some people say that some have made pacts with the devil. They have exchanged their soul for success.

If you're going to have success God's way, you'll never have to exchange your soul in order to do it. You will never have to put down God's Word or godly living in order for you to be successful.

If you come to the place where that is the condition and the criteria to earn success, you have to tell yourself that that's too high of a price. The Bible says that although Lot was reaping multiple blessings by being in the Lord's favor, he was still not satisfied. He looked at the plains of Sodom and travelled there.

And if you look at Lot's life, he lost everything. He lost his prosperity; he lost his success; he lost his good name; he lost his wife; he lost his children; he lost everything. And all this transpired because he wanted to step outside of God's will for him.

Be sure to always be asking yourself, "Am I being greedy? Am I trying to step outside God's will? Am I dissatisfied with God's blessings in my life?"

God wants you to be successful, but He'll never let you sell your soul in order to do it.

CHAPTER NINE

Key Ingredient 8: Association

Proverbs 27:17 says, "Iron sharpens iron; so a man sharpeneth the countenance of his friend." In other words, the people you hang out with will influence how you respond to life in general.

The people you associate with should sharpen your disposition. Your friends are there to help build your countenance. One version says that your face reflects the attitude of your heart. Someone can look at your face and see what's going on inside.

So if your friends or your associates are not making your countenance better, you need to check who you're hanging out with. The NIV says, "Like iron sharpens iron, so one person sharpens another."

It's important that the people you hang out with are sharpening you. That means that they should be helping your life develop in a way that brings God glory.

In the Message Bible it says, "You use steel to sharpen to steel." In other words, God uses other people in your life to help build you. And then it says, "One friend sharpens another friend."

If the people you're hanging out with are not adding to your life, then you're hanging out with the wrong people and God may not be able to use you in the building of success His way.

If you're hanging with people who are tearing you down, you're hanging with blunt instruments, not sharp ones.

Friends and associates should build one another not hinder and tear down one another. If you're hanging with people who are tearing you down, you're hanging with blunt instruments, not sharp ones. God wants us to hang around people that help sharpen our lives to be used for the Kingdom of God.

1 Corinthians 15:33 says, "Do not be deceived. Evil communication corrupts good manners."

The Bible says, "Evil association corrupts good morals." That's a powerful verse from the Apostle Paul. The word communicate is koinonia which means to fellowship. Who you're fellowshipping with can affect what you say, both right and wrong.

I know that some people don't think that's true. But it doesn't take much for you to jump on the bandwagon—

whether for good or bad—when your friends are doing it.

If you were to take a glass of the purest water, and dump a teaspoon of dirt into it, you will notice the change instantly. That pure glass of water will become contaminated, cloudy and dark.

It is generally easier for bad morals to corrupt good ones than for good morals to convert bad morals.

But if you take a teaspoon of the pure water and drop it in a glass of pure dirt, all you get is mud. The same goes for people. It is generally easier for bad morals to corrupt good ones than for good morals to convert bad morals.

If you constantly hang around ungodliness, you're going to have a good, long time of ministry before you can influence and change anyone for the good or the kingdom of God.

But if you're not careful, you'll begin to be negatively influenced by their corrupt behavior. You'll begin to tell their dirty jokes, cuss, talk crudely, and all kinds of evil sins that you normally wouldn't commit on your own.

Even if you think you're strong, take heed lest you fall. In 2 Peter 2:7, it says that Lot went down to the city of Sodom, and when he got there, the city was lush and beautiful. He sat at the gates with the elders, which implies that the elders welcomed him into their city.

They said, "You seem like a good man. Why don't you sit at the gate and give counsel?" Now, the city was full of wickedness and corruption. At the end of 2 Peter 2:7, it says, "But just Lot vexing his soul with the filthy communication of those in Sodom, he lost everything."

Hebrews warns that we must not forsake to gather with other believers until we see the end time approaching. In other words, believers should be around believers.

In other words, Lot never influenced the people of Sodom, but they influenced him. As you can see by the story of Lot, it is very important who you associate with. In Hebrews, it warns that we must not forsake to gather with other believers until we see the end time approaching. In other words, believers should be around believers.

Now, I'm not saying that we should reject unbelievers. But if we are only around them, and you're not strong in the faith, it's possible their bad morals will corrupt you. Being around true believers should uplift you, they'll pray for you, motivate you, and encourage you. Being around them should energize your faith and make you pursue God's call on your life with all the more vigor.

Let me ask you a question: If you were on trial for being a Christian, would there be enough evidence to convict you? It's a sad testimony if someone at your work said, "I didn't even know he went to church. He never talks about anything like that."

Association determines your level of success in God's way. In other words, God can use the people you hang out with to help move you to where it is that He needs you to be.

Choose to Fly with Eagles

In other words, you can choose to soar high above everything that's going on. The choice is yours. Or you can choose to fly with the buzzards. Buzzards are scavengers. They fly but not very long.

We are products of where we are today based on decisions and people that we associated with yesterday.

Buzzards fly just long enough to spot some dead thing, then they swoop down and get in the middle of the mess. Eagles soar in high places and they only come down to a low place in order to get prey. Once they get their prey, they carry it back to the high place.

You'll never see an eagle eating on the ground. But you see buzzards eating on the ground all the time. So the question is: Do you have the ability to soar?

I'm sure you've heard the phrase, "Birds of a feather flock together." But those same birds also arrive at the same destination. If you don't believe me, look at birds when they migrate at the appropriate season. Birds do not migrate by themselves. They flock in a pack and they head in a particular direction. And the direction they head is the destination that they all end up in. So if you want to know what your future looks like, assess who you're hanging out with.

Now, I'm not saying that everybody you hang out with is bad. Who knows? You may be the bad influencer. We are products of where we are today based on decisions and people that we associated with yesterday. Many of us have instructors, Sunday school teachers, and men and women of God who have positively and profoundly impacted our lives to cause us to be who we are today.

We have to be careful about what we take in.

Early in my life when I was in my twenties, I had the pleasure of meeting a particular person and working around him for 7 years, and he has influenced me to be the best me I can be. He is the one who made me see that you could live godly and make it as an African-

American male. Prior to meeting him, most of my examples that I had seen were not being successful God's way. It made me question whether I could really be a productive person in society.

Many of us have models. Often most of our role models we get from television. All television is doing, is telling you someone else's vision. And if you look at what they offer on television for the African- American population, it's not good. I'm tired of seeing movies about prison, violence, gang-banging, hanging and partying. Very little is constructive. Many of the commercials and the sponsors promote alcohol and tobacco.

And if that kind of television is your predominant model, your decision-making is poor.

If you'll notice, the news on what goes on around the world is mostly not positive. They're either going to show you a movie that's about prison or they'll put somebody on TV that will make you laugh. And then they're going to propagate some kind of alcoholic beverage for your life. I believe the networks have a moral responsibility to uphold good, ethical and moral values.

Highly successful people don't just hang out. They have a regimen that causes them to be disciplined and productive.

We have to be careful about what we take in. David said, "I made a covenant with God that I would set my eyes on nothing that would cause my heart to be turned from you."

We must protect the eye-gate and the ear-gate because out of the heart flows the issues of life. And the entrance point is your ears and eyes. It's not what a man puts in his mouth that defileth him; it's what comes out of his mouth.

How to Glean or Build Relationships with Successful People

It's not easy to get into the life of someone who is successful. Because successful people are not necessarily looking for friends. Because successful people understand the law of association. They have a very tightknit circle. And you do not break in to their inner circle. They keep you on the peripheral—until they have sized you up and seen if you have anything of value to add to their sphere of influence. If you do not have anything to add, they see you merely as an associate at a distance. They do not see you as a close and trusted friend.

If you want to get into upper- level management, you are not going to get there with your pants sagging.

Highly successful people don't just hang out. They have a regimen that causes them to be disciplined and productive. There's an old saying that says: *If you want to be one of them, you must walk like 'em, talk like 'em, look like 'em.*

That means if you want to be where they are you need to fit in. If you're a young man, you are not going to get there with your pants sagging.

Three Ways to Build Relationships with Successful People

1. Learn to read their thoughts

How do you do that? By reading their books and listening to their tapes or CD's. You may not be able to get into their inner circle to hang out, but having access to their thoughts and philosophies, you can become informed to where you're thinking on their level.

2. Attend the same places they frequent and network with their group type.

Now that you have read their books and listened to their tapes, it's time to run in the same circles in which they run. That way, if the opportunity presents itself to meet them, you now can have a discussion or conversation on their level. And who knows, with favor from God, perhaps a relationship will emerge.

3. Pray for divine access and favor

Please notice the priority level by which I listed these three points. Please notice that you had to do the work before you tried to pray for it to work. Sometimes we as Christians pray for favor, but when we get there, we don't know anything about the people that we need to meet. We don't know anything about who it is and what they say and what they do. We don't know anything about the places that they hang, but we just bump into them at Walmart.

I don't need to pray for divine access and favor if I don't know anything that they think about, talk about, write about or go to any of the places that they hang out.

We must stop asking for divine favor and divine access when we haven't done the necessary homework where we can articulate on that level. Sometimes God wants to open doors, but we don't have the keys in order to give us access.

So now that I've done what I needed, I'm praying for a divine impartation where God sets me in their path and now when I get set in their path, they take notice that I've got something intelligent to add.

And by that I mean, I am informed on the situations and the subject matters by which they may be speaking of. How did I get informed? I read their books. I heard their tapes. And I know something about the subject matter. Then I'm able to ask eloquently so that I don't look like a baboon or a fool.

God uses people to do great things because they were informed. Then God gave them access. Many of us know about Nehemiah. Nehemiah was the cupbearer to the king. Do you think Nehemiah got to be in that position by knowing nothing about royalty? Do you think that God would've given Nehemiah favor with the king in order to build the wall if Nehemiah didn't know anything about checks and balances?

We must stop asking for divine favor and divine access when we haven't done the necessary homework where we can articulate on that level. Sometimes God wants to open doors, but we don't have the keys in order to give us access.

Great people don't give you access to their circle if they don't know that you're going to make them look good. So what do you need to do? Learn how to preach to a hundred before you can learn to preach to thousands.

Great people don't give you access to their circle if they don't know that you're going to make them look good. So what do you need to do? Learn how to preach to a hundred before you can learn to preach to thousands. Learn how to supervise the one on your team before you learn how to supervise a team of a hundred. I don't care if you work in the mail room and you have one person under you, learn how to lead well.

Some of us are not ready to associate with others. Maybe every morning you're as mean as an old wet hen. Maybe you have trouble with people on the road every morning when you drive to work. Nothing ever pleases you. You don't like your makeup; you don't like the song they are playing on the radio; you don't like the weather.

It's amazing what you can get done with a smile and a hello.

You don't like the folks in the other car who keep cutting you off. You don't like the direction that you're going because traffic is slow. You arrive at work mad because you can't park close to the door. Now it will take you longer to walk to your office.

You walk in. It starts to rain. Your hair begins to curl up. By the time you get to your desk, you tell everybody, "Don't talk to me; just leave me alone." And everybody knows if you haven't had 4 cups of coffee and it isn't 12 o'clock, don't say hello.

If this describes you, then you're sure to be running off people who want to associate with you. It's amazing what you can get done with a smile and a hello. Folks whose day is not even going well will walk by your desk because they just know that you will say something to pep them up.

I'm telling you the truth. Folks learn pretty quickly who to avoid early in the morning on the job. If no one ever talks to you in the morning, maybe it's because you're snarly in the morning.

Assess who's around you. Assess not only who has influence in your circle but assess who you have influenced in that circle.

I'll never forget in my first church when I was speaking, there was this one lady who came up to me and said, "I just love those sermons that you preach."

I said, "What do you mean? What sermons?" She said, "The ones that just go right over my head and hit the person behind me square between the eyes."

What she was saying was that everything you say is always for the person behind me. You have to be careful. Make sure that you do inventory. Assess who's around you. Assess not only who has influence in your circle but assess who you have influenced in that circle. And then after you assess the situation, pray about it.

Then begin to administer. Begin to administrate some things in your life. Maybe there's a person that you love, but you know you shouldn't hang out with them as much because they're causing you to go to the wrong places.

Maybe you're married and they're single and they want you to go hang out with them in the single hang out place. That's the wrong person for you to be hanging out with. You don't have to end the friendship, but you have to be careful. But you can't go where they go because what they're looking for is not what you should be looking for.

Once you've done all these things, you can attentively allow the Holy Spirit to instruct you in you how He desires to make you successful.

Then, and only then, will you start finding success *God's* way. My prayer is that God's promised best will be yours!

Acknowledgements

My deepest heartfelt appreciation to my Lord and Savior Jesus Christ who has prospered me and given me the godly success I have dreamed of. I would like to thank my mother Barbara Metcalf for believing and challenging me to be the best that God could have me to be. To my mother-in-law Nettie Kelly who has counseled me on being sensitive to the voice of the Holy Spirit over these 20 years of ministry. To my 96-year-old aunt Mamie McAllister that spoke the words "If God told you to go to Arkansas then you best be on your way." To Russell Wendell Nelson Jr. for being a mentor to a young man who did not know he could do things the right way and be financially successful legitimately. To Bishop IV Hilliard who has mentored me from afar and about faith and how to present the Word of God as a teacher in the body of Christ. To Bishop Napoleon Rhodes who spoke into my life as a father and ordained me to the Bishopric. Lastly, but mostly, to my beautiful wife Pleshette and our four lovely children Leslie, Dinah, Joshua and Jordan, who have supported me in every endeavor of life with love, prayer, and faith. I love you more than anything in this world and I thank you from the bottom of my heart for believing in me. I've only named a few and not all of those that are dear to me and have invested in my life. It's my desire that every reader will examine their life and apply these principles, so they too may experience success God's way.

— Bishop John L. Benford

About The Author

John L. Benford is the founder of the international television ministry, *Faith Time with Bishop*. He and his wife, Pleshette, formed Valley Harvest Ministries of Rogers, Arkansas in 1998, where he's senior pastor. He was elected into the Bishopric of The Convention of Covenanting Church of Los Angeles, California in 2000, where he serves as the fifth Jurisdictional Bishop.

He and his wife have been married for 24 years and have been blessed with four beautiful children. His teaching ministry has lead thousands to Christ and helped countless others to achieve the abundant life that Christ spoke of in John 10:10b.

About SermonToBook.Com

SermonToBook.com began with a simple belief: that sermons should be touching lives, *not* collecting dust. That's why we turn sermons into high-quality books that are accessible to people all over the globe.

Turning your sermon or sermon series into a book exposes more people to God's Word, better equips you for counseling, accelerates future sermon prep, adds credibility to your ministry, and even helps make ends meet during tight times.

John 21:25 tells us that the world itself couldn't contain the books that would be written about the work of Jesus Christ. Our mission is to try anyway. Because, in Heaven, there will no longer be a need for sermons or books. Our time is now.

If God so leads you, we'd love to work with you on your sermon or sermon series.

Visit www.sermontobook.com to learn more.

YOUR *PROBLEMS*
HAVE *PURPOSE*

UNDERSTANDING GOD'S PLAN
FOR YOUR LIFE

STEVE BOZEMAN

All Problems in your past, present and future have a Purpose to fulfill in your life! The problems you are dealing with are leaving you frustrated, depressed and feeling like God has abandoned you. You've been praying for relief and you've even tried to borrow relief, but nothing is working. You constantly question, "Why all of these problems, God?"

Your Problems Have Purpose is an engaging book, full of practical life-application principles including:

- Discovering who you are in Christ
- Growing in God's purpose for you
- Learning how to overcome the fact that brokenness hurts
- Submitting to God's will for your life and living successfully

Additionally you'll learn...

- Exactly how God uses your problems to develop your purpose
- Why God uses problems to protect you from yourself
- What your purpose cost God

Discover how important your problems are to God's purposeful plan for your life, and how the RIGHT perspective makes all the difference!

Purchase today on Amazon.com!

SPENDING
TIME WITH
GOD

GOD'S DAILY PRESENCE FULFILLS YOUR GREATEST PURPOSE

JAMES THOMAS

Spending time with God is one of the greatest privileges you have in life. Greater than your public worship, greater than your spiritual gifts, greater than preaching and teaching the gospel. When you commit yourself to spending time with your Heavenly Father on a daily basis, it will change your life. Period.

God wants to spend time with you, not because He's lonely, but because you so desperately need His daily presence in order to fulfill your greatest purpose.

In *Spending Time With God*, you'll learn super practical ways to draw near to your Heavenly Father and experience life-changing transformation as He draws near to you. For starters, you'll discover:

• 4 disciplines that motivate and inspire spending time with God

• The incredible impact of spending time with God

• Required elements for spending time with God

• The power of prayer and praise while spending time with God

Prepare yourself for the spectacular. Because when you experience God's daily presence, He fulfills your greatest purpose.

Purchase today on Amazon.com!

SCOTT SANDERS

HOLY SPIRIT TRAINING

DISCOVER THE PREDOMINANT
DIVINE POWER ON EARTH

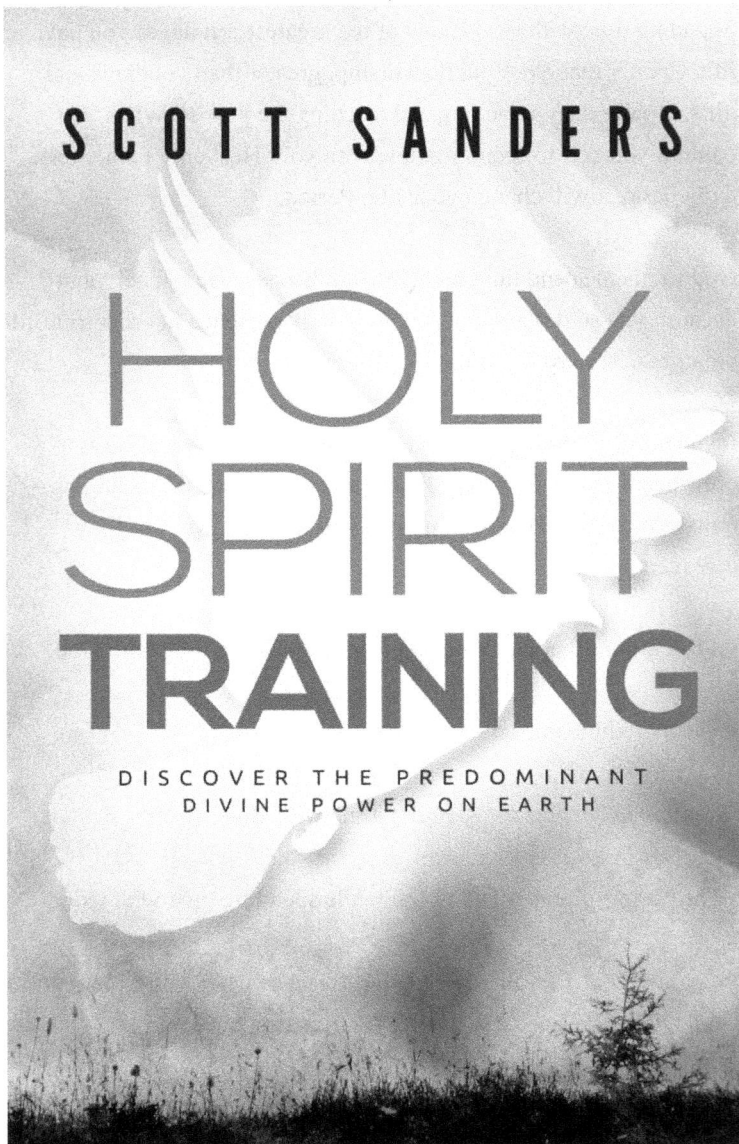

If you've ever wondered if you've completely missed the purpose and ministry of the Holy Spirit, then this book might be a shocker for you.

There's a big difference between knowing the characteristics of the Spirit and knowing the Spirit as a person. The Holy Spirit is the predominant divine power on earth right now. But do you truly know Him?

In Holy Spirit Training, you'll train your senses to know there's more going on than what your eyes can see, discover how the Spirit is the key to accessing the "things" God has prepared for you, and learn exactly who the Spirit is and how He works. Get ready to discover:

• The role of the Holy Spirit in your life

• How to pick up the signals of the Holy Spirit

• How to follow and be led by the Holy Spirit

• How to partner with the Holy Spirit to manifest things on earth

Don't hesitate another day. Decide now to truly know the Holy Spirit and let Him guide you through life and put some *super* on your *natural*!

GOD
LOVES ME

*How A Revelation Of God's Love For
You Can Revolutionize Your Life*

ANDRE MITCHELL

In the subtitle of this book, I chose the two themes of revelation and revolution because as I meditated on God loving me specifically and personally … it transformed my Christianity.

Like stated in Romans 12:2, my mind was renewed and my Christian walk revolutionized. It dawned on me that my sins alone put Jesus on that cross. Had the world not consisted of billions of people and instead the world only consisted of little ole me, He still would have had to die. My personal sin debt was enormous. I was born in sin and shaped in iniquity. There were no two ways around it. Yet, He did what He did because He loved me. Always had, and always will. He loves me.

It is for this revelation alone that I wrote this book: so that you too can be revolutionized, like I was and still am being because it's a journey you never exit. Or ever want to. So I invite you to join me in a discovery of revelation and revolution as God unveils what it means to be loved by the Creator of the universe!

www.ingramcontent.com/pod-product-compliance
Lightning Source LLC
Chambersburg PA
CBHW061831040426
42447CB00012B/2922